HOW WE USE MAPS AND GLOBES

By
Muriel Stanek

Illustrated by
Frank Larocco

Photos
John Gorecki

BENEFIC PRESS · CHICAGO

Primary Supplementary

Social Studies Program

How Series

HOW HOSPITALS HELP US
HOW SCHOOLS HELP US
HOW WE CELEBRATE OUR SPRING HOLIDAYS
HOW WE GET OUR MAIL
HOW WEATHER AFFECTS US
HOW FAMILIES LIVE TOGETHER
HOW DOCTORS HELP US

HOW AIRPLANES HELP US
HOW WE CELEBRATE OUR FALL HOLIDAYS
HOW WE GET OUR CLOTHING
HOW WE TRAVEL ON WATER
HOW FOODS ARE PRESERVED
HOW WE GET OUR DAIRY FOODS
HOW WE USE MAPS AND GLOBES

HOW WE GET OUR CLOTH
HOW WE GET OUR SHELTER
HOW WE TRAVEL ON LAND
HOW PEOPLE LIVE IN THE BIG CITY
HOW COMMUNICATION HELPS US
HOW PRINTING HELPS US
HOW PEOPLE EARN AND USE MONEY

Copyright 1968 by Benefic Press
All Rights Reserved
Printed in the United States of America

Library of Congress
Number 67-30763

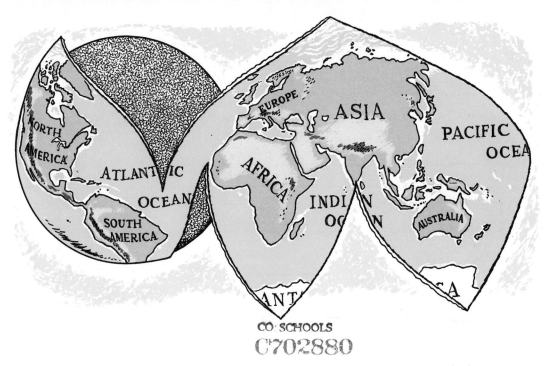

CONTENTS

The earth as spacemen see it.

HOW GLOBES HELP US

This is a globe. A globe is a ball made to look like a very small earth.

The earth is almost round. A globe is round, too.

The earth turns. A globe will turn, too.

What does a globe show?

The earth is made up of land and water. On a globe, water is always shown in blue. Land is shown in other colors.

Let's make believe that we could put all the land in one place on the earth. The rest of the earth could be water.

We would see that the earth has three times more water than land.

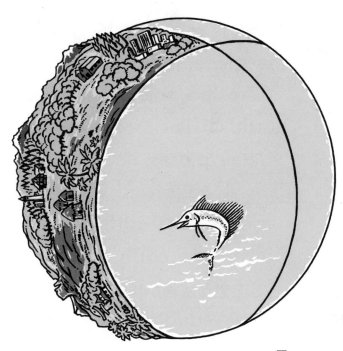

If you were to go as far north as you could on the earth, you would at last come to the North Pole. If you went as far south as you could go, you would come to the South Pole. You would not find real poles coming from the earth. The North Pole and the South Pole are just places.

A globe has a North Pole and a South Pole, too.

Halfway between the North Pole and the South Pole, there is a line. This line goes all the way around the globe. It is called the equator.

Like the poles, the equator is just a place on the earth. It is not a real line on the real earth.

Most places near the equator are warm all year. It is always cold at the poles of the earth.

Half of the earth is called a hemisphere. The half of the earth north of the equator is the Northern Hemisphere. The half of the earth south of the equator is the Southern Hemisphere.

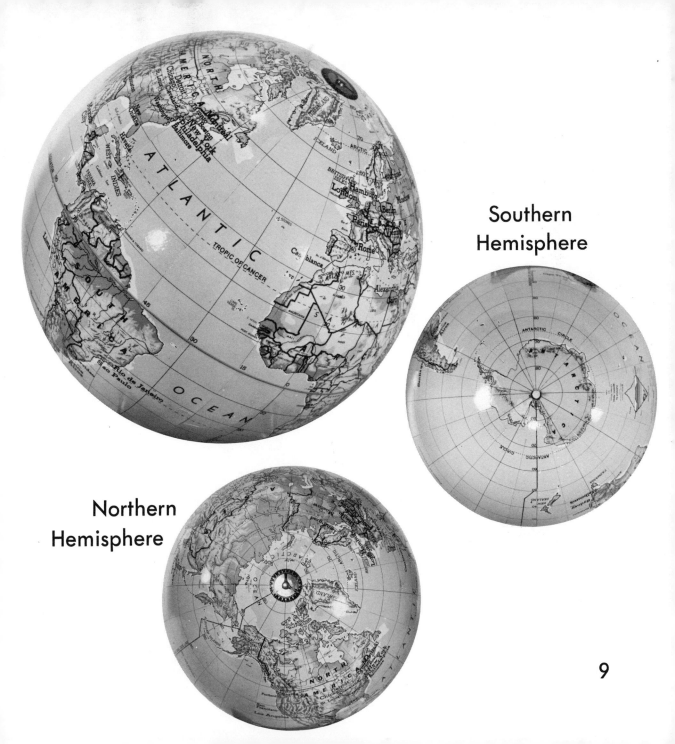

Southern
Hemisphere

Northern
Hemisphere

9

You can show other hemispheres. This shows us the Western Hemisphere.

This shows the Eastern Hemisphere.

HOW MAPS HELP US

What is a map?

A map is a drawing of all of the earth or of any part of the earth.

This map shows a small part of the earth.

TEXAS

This map shows more of the earth.

ARIZONA NEW MEXICO TEXAS

11

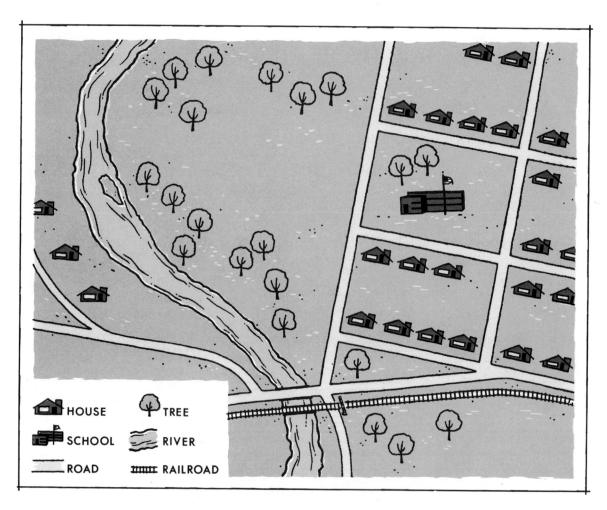

HOUSE · TREE · SCHOOL · RIVER · ROAD · RAILROAD

What do maps show?

Maps can show many kinds of things. One kind of map may show things that are on the earth.

12

Maps can show things to help people who travel.

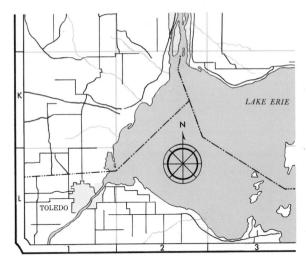

Maps can show the way birds go when they fly north or south for the season.

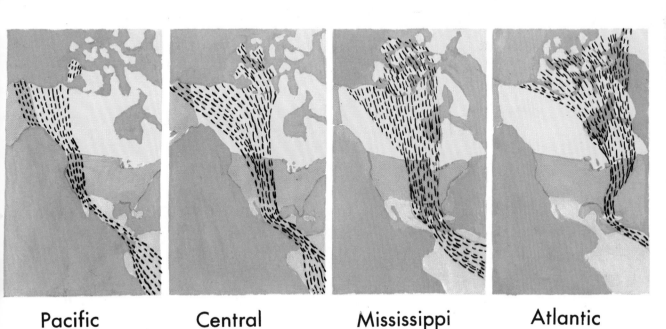

| Pacific flyway | Central flyway | Mississippi flyway | Atlantic flyway |

UNITED STATES
POLITICAL

Scale – 1:14,889,610 or
1 inch to 235 miles

0   100   250   500

STATE OF ALASKA
1/2 Scale of main map

PACIFIC OCEAN

PRINCIPAL ISLANDS OF THE
STATE OF HAWAII
18-1/2 Scale of main map

PACIFIC OCEAN

Victoria · Vancouver
WASH.
Seattle
Olympia
Portland · Columbia · OREG.
Salem
IDAHO
Helena
MONT.
Boise
NEV.
UTAH
Salt Lake City
Carson City
Sacramento
San Francisco
CALIF.
Los Angeles
San Diego
Phoenix
ARIZ.
Colorado R.
Gila R.
El Paso
MEXICO
Santa Fe
Albuquerque
N. MEX.
Denver
COLO.
Cheyenne
WYO.
Edmunton
B.C.
ALB.
Regina
SASK.
MAN.
Winnipeg
N. DAK.
Bismarck
S. DAK.
Pierre
Missouri R.
NEBR.
Lincoln
Omaha
IOWA
Des Moines
MINN.
Duluth
WIS.
St. Paul
Minneapolis
Madison
KAN.
Topeka
Kansas City
St. Louis
MO.
Jefferson City
OKLA.
Oklahoma City
ARK.
Little Rock
TEX.
Dallas
LA.
Baton Rouge
Austin
Houston
San Antonio
Rio Grande
PACIFIC OCEAN

STATE OF ALASKA
BROOKS RANGE
Nome
Yukon River
Fairbanks
Anchorage
Juneau
Ketchikan
Gulf of Alaska
Bering Sea
ALEUTIAN ISLANDS

KAUAI
NIIHAU
OAHU
Honolulu
MOLOKAI
LANAI
MAUI
KAHOOLAWE
HAWAII

This is a
map that
shows all
the land of
the United
States.

How are maps and globes different?

A map is flat. A globe is round.

A map can be used to show a small part of the earth. The map can show many things from that part of the earth. There is not enough room on a globe to show all the things a map can show.

You can carry a map with you.

Because a globe is round, it can give a true picture of land and water bodies as they are on the earth. Because they are flat, maps cannot give as true a picture of the whole earth.

A globe can help us learn how the earth moves. Maps cannot do this.

WHAT ARE DIRECTIONS?

Direction is the way something is pointing or moving. People may point in a direction. Signs may point in a direction, too.

Directions are shown on maps, too. Most maps have an arrow that points in the direction of the North Pole.

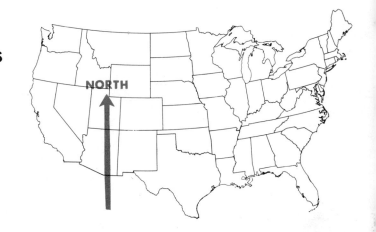

North on the globe is in the direction of the North Pole, too.

NORTH

WEST 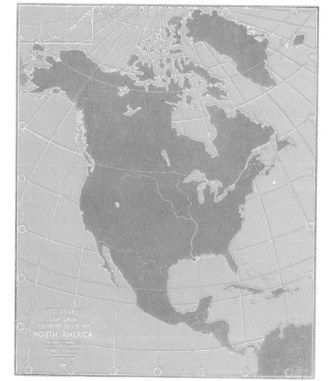 EAST

SOUTH

On most maps, north is at the top. When north is at the top, south is at the bottom. South is always in the direction of the South Pole on a map and on a globe, too.

20

With north at the top of the map, east will be in the direction of the right side of the map. West will be to the left side.

East is to the right and west to the left on a globe, too.

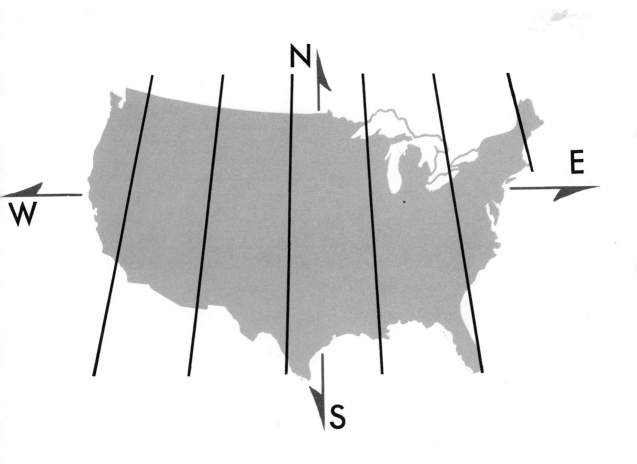

On the real earth, north is always in the direction of the North Pole, too. Sometimes we use a compass to help us find north. When we know which direction is north, we can find all the other directions, too.

Sometimes the direction-finder on a map is drawn to look almost like a compass.

Northeast is the direction between north and east.
Northwest is the direction between north and west.
Southeast is the direction between south and east.
Southwest is the direction between south and west.

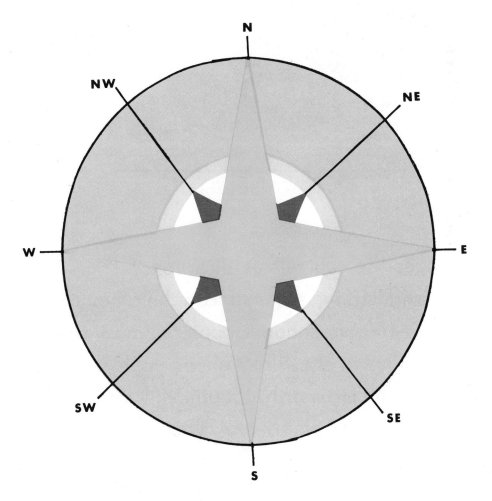

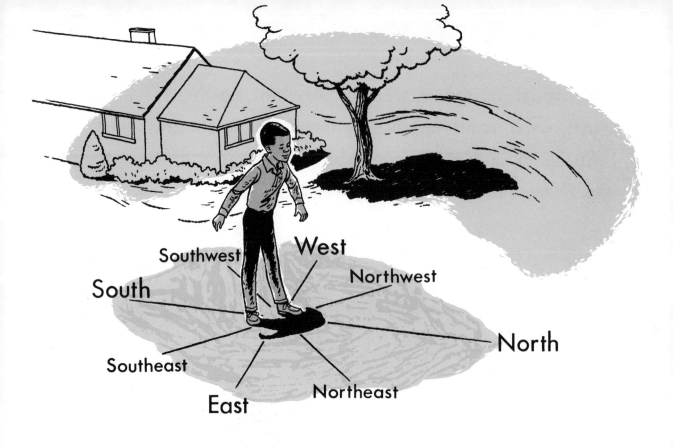

How does the sun tell us directions?

On a bright day, the sun can help you find direction. At noon, shadows point almost true north. Looking in the direction of your shadow, you will be facing north. South will be at your back, east to your right, and west to your left.

How does the North Star tell direction?

At night, the North Star can show us which direction is north. The North Star is seen in the sky right over the North Pole.

People have used the North Star to find direction at night for years and years.

What are longitude and latitude?

People who make maps and globes may draw lines running from the North Pole to the South Pole. These are lines of longitude.

They may also draw lines all the way around the globe north and south of the equator. These are lines of latitude.

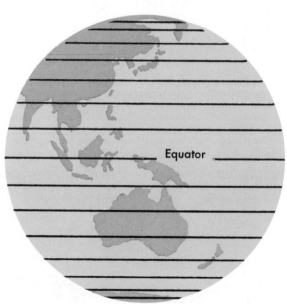

Equator

The lines of latitude
and longitude are given
numbers.

If we know the latitude and the longitude, we
can find any place we want on a map or on a globe.

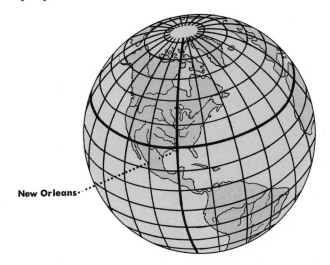

New Orleans

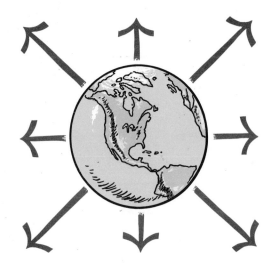

What are up and down?

Up is the direction away from the earth. It is not the same as north.

All of these arrows are going up from the earth.

Down is the direction toward the earth. It is not the same as south.

All of these arrows are going down to the earth.

28

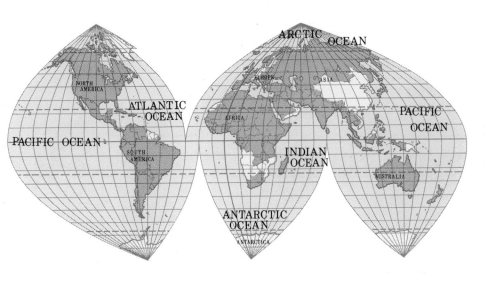

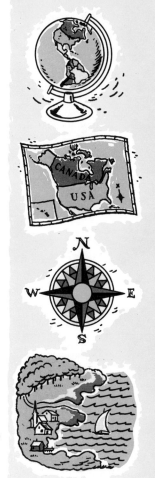

LAND AND WATER ON GLOBES AND MAPS

What is an ocean?

Looking at a globe or a map of the world, we see that the earth is covered by many bodies of water. The five very large bodies of water are oceans.

An ocean is a great body of salt water.

29

Big ships carry many people across the ocean at one time. It takes about five days for a ship to go across the Atlantic Ocean today.

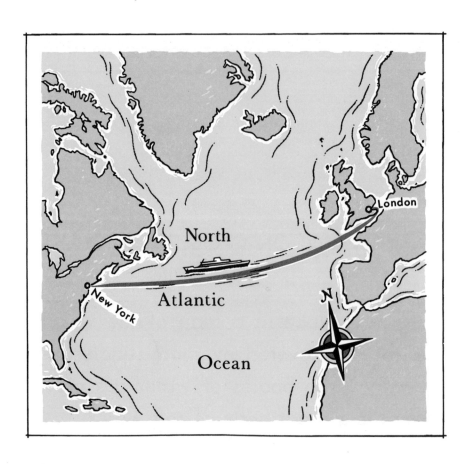

What is a lake?

A body of water with land around it is called a lake. Lakes are shown in blue on maps and globes.

Some lakes are large. Others are small.

Five very large lakes in North America are called the Great Lakes.

Many cities are near lakes.

Chicago

Detroit

Buffalo

What is a river?

Maps and globes show rivers, too. Only the large rivers of the earth can be shown on a globe.

Maps can show large rivers and small ones, too.

What is a coast?

A coast is the place where the land and the ocean come together. Not all coasts look the same.

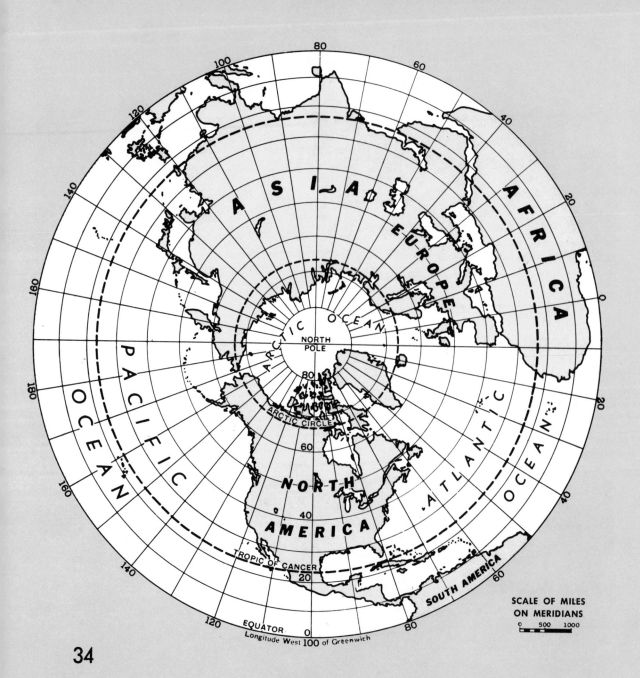

SCALE OF MILES
ON MERIDIANS

0   500   1000

34

How is land shown?
Land bodies of the
earth are shown on maps
and globes in colors
other than blue. The
largest land bodies of
the earth are called
continents. There are
seven continents in all.
They are all different
sizes and shapes.

Most of the United
States is on the continent
of North America.

An island is a body of
land that has water all
the way around it.

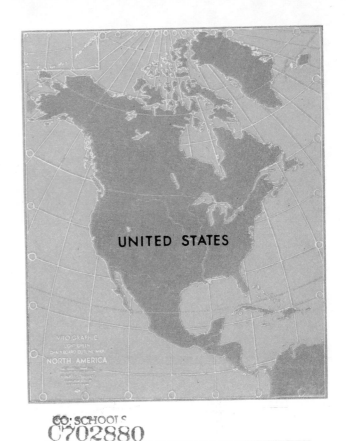

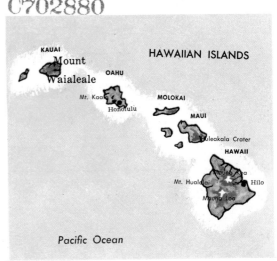

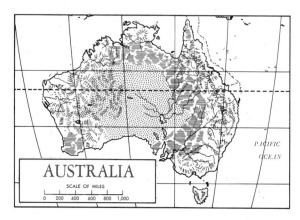

How are mountains shown?

Mountains are shown on maps and globes in a number of ways.

Sometimes little lines show mountains.

Many times a brown color shows where mountains are. Here we can see all the mountains of the United States and Canada by looking at the brown coloring.

CANADA

New York

Chicago

Los Angeles

Denver

San Francisco

UNITED STATES

Atlanta

MEXICO

USING THE GLOBE TO LEARN ABOUT NIGHT AND DAY AND THE SEASONS

How does the earth rotate?

The earth is always turning. We say that it rotates on its axis. Rotate means turn around. The earth's axis is a make-believe line through its center. We can see where the earth's axis is by looking at a globe.

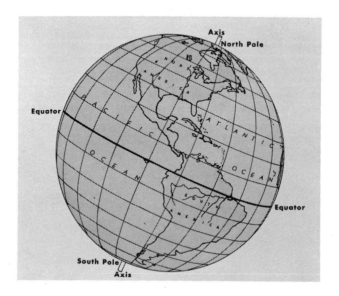

What are night and day?

The earth rotates on its axis once every twenty-four hours. This means that it turns all the way around every twenty-four hours. The earth turns from east to west.

As the earth turns, we have day and night. The half of the earth that is turned toward the sun has day. The half of the earth that is turned away from the sun has night.

We can use a globe to see how day and night come to the earth. The half of the globe turned toward the light has day. The half of the globe in the shadow has night.

It is fun to watch your shadow. Early in the morning and late in the day, your shadow is long. That is because the sun is seen as low in the sky at those times.

At noon, your shadow is very short. That is because the sun is seen as high in the sky.

Early Morning

Noon

Late Afternoon

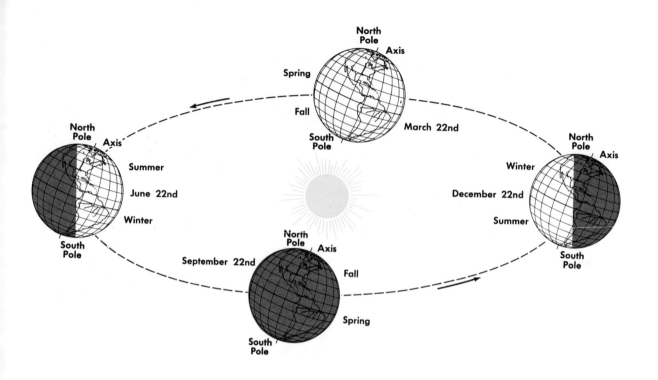

How does the earth travel?

The earth rotates on its axis once every twenty-four hours. But it is also moving in another way. It is traveling around the sun, too. It takes the earth one year to travel all the way around the sun. We have four seasons as the earth travels around the sun.

42

HOW MAPS SHOW DISTANCE

What does scale mean on a map?

A map may show a continent or all of the world. A map may show just the block where you live. A small space or line on a map may really be a mile or more on a real street. The scale of a map shows the distance on the earth for each inch on the map.

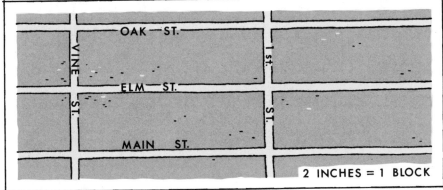

2 INCHES = 1 BLOCK

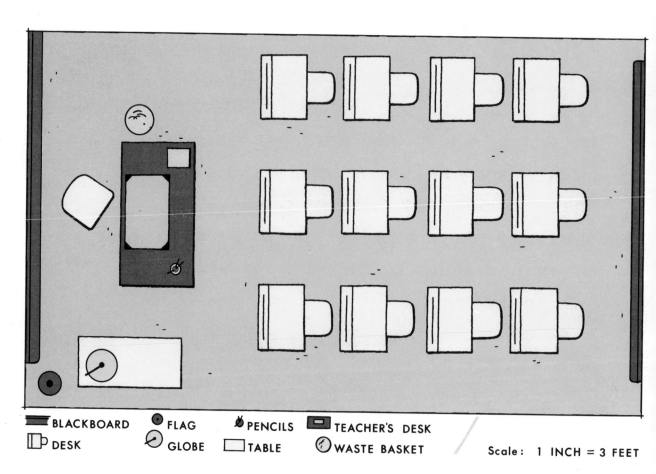

BLACKBOARD   FLAG   PENCILS   TEACHER'S DESK
DESK   GLOBE   TABLE   WASTE BASKET   Scale: 1 INCH = 3 FEET

We can make a map of a room, too. It might look like this. A map is drawn as if you were looking down from above. That way, all of the room can be shown. On this map, one inch stands for three feet.

The block where you live may have houses and a street. But a community takes in streets, homes, and many other things, too. Here is a map of one community. On this map, one inch stands for two blocks.

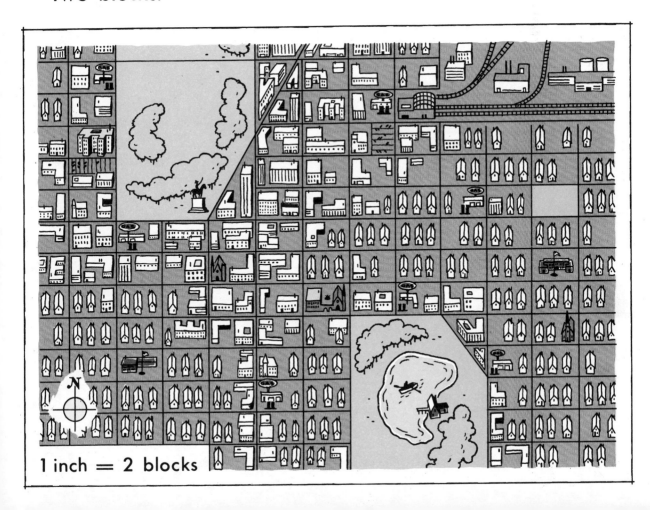

1 inch = 2 blocks

This map shows the fifty states of the United States. Alaska and Hawaii are in the small boxes. You will find the state where you live. You may find the city, too. But you will not find your community. Each inch on this map stands for many miles. Most communities are too small to show.

Maps and globes can show us many things. We can learn about land and water on the earth. We can learn about direction and distance by looking at maps and globes.

A map is good because it can show many more things about parts of the earth than a globe can show.

A globe is good because it can show true shapes and sizes of land and water bodies of the earth.

VOCABULARY ANALYSIS

The suggested reading level of this book is second grade. The twenty-eight words listed below in roman type are second grade words; those three shown in italic type are above second-grade level.

The social-studies words listed at the bottom of the page are considered basic to the understanding of the subject matter and have not been classified according to reading level. All the words are in alphabetical order, and the number indicates the page on which the word first appears.

almost 5	*fifty* 46	learn 15	real 8
also 42	flat 14	low 41	
arrow 19			same 28
	halfway 9	means 38	seven 34
believe 7	hours 39		ships 30
between 9			short 41
bottom 20	*inch* 43	noon 24	
		numbers 27	toward 39
different 14	large 29		travel 13
drawn 9	late 41	part 11	true 15
		pointing 18	twenty-four 39

Social Studies Terms

axis 38	Eastern 10	north 8	seasons 13
	equator 8	Northeast 22	shadows 24
block 43		North Star 25	shapes 35
bodies 29	globe 5	Northwest 22	sizes 34
			south 8
center 9	hemisphere 10		Southeast 22
coast 33		oceans 29	Southwest 22
community 46	island 34		space 43
compass 23		pole 8	states 46
continent 34	lake 31		street 43
	land 6		
direction 18	latitude 26	rivers 32	water 6
distance 43	longitude 26	rotate 38	west 21
			Western 10
earth 5	maps 11	salt 29	world 43
east 19	mile 43	scale 3	
	mountains 36		